T0368812

SERIES 205

In this book, we will look at frosty woodlands,
clear wintry skies and snowy tracks, as we
explore the beauty of the winter.

LADYBIRD BOOKS
UK | USA | Canada | Ireland | Australia
India | New Zealand | South Africa
Ladybird Books is part of the Penguin Random House group of companies
whose addresses can be found at global.penguinrandomhouse.com.
www.penguin.co.uk   www.puffin.co.uk   www.ladybird.co.uk

First published 2020
002
Copyright © Ladybird Books Ltd, 2020
Printed in Italy
A CIP catalogue record for this book is available from the British Library
ISBN: 978–0–241–41622–8
All correspondence to:
Ladybird Books
Penguin Random House Children's
One Embassy Gardens, 8 Viaduct Gardens
London SW11 7BW

What to Look For in **Winter**

A Ladybird Book

Written by Elizabeth Jenner

Illustrated by Natasha Durley

Winter is coming

Early on a dark December morning, there is a chill in the air. As the sun rises over the grassland, it catches the frost on the grasses and teasels, making them sparkle.

Frost is created on still, cold nights, when the water vapour in the air turns to droplets and then land on solid surfaces and plants. As the air temperature drops below zero degrees Celsius (32°F), the water droplets start to freeze into ice crystals. This frozen blanket is called "ground frost".

The spikier frost often found on plants is created differently. This "hoar frost" appears after particularly cold nights, when the water vapour in the air comes into contact with surfaces that are already at a temperature below freezing. Ice crystals form instantly and, as more water vapour freezes, the ice builds in layers to create feathery structures.

These goldfinches are breaking through the hoar frost on the teasel heads to gain access to their morning meal. The prickly cone-like dead heads of the teasel plant are full of tasty seeds, and in winter, when food is scarce and the days are cold, these rich, high-fat seeds are one of the goldfinches' best sources of fuel.

Drift seeds

When walking on a wintry beach, look out for strange, glossy objects lying on the sand. These are drift seeds, and many will have travelled hundreds of miles from tropical places, carried by the ocean's waves.

Some tropical trees and plants produce large, hard seeds that float. The seeds fall from pods into nearby water sources, and some find their way to the sea. They can then travel across the oceans and end up on much colder shores.

Drift seeds come in all shapes and sizes. This brown "sea heart" is the seed from a giant plant called the "monkey ladder", found in Central America. Each heart-shaped seed is around 5 centimetres (2 in.) wide. Historically, sea hearts discovered on the coast of Ireland were placed under pillows, to ward off supernatural forces.

The shiny, grey marbles are nicker seeds, or "nickernuts", and they come from the warri tree in the Caribbean. Historically, when they washed up on the Scottish Hebrides islands, the locals would use them to make necklaces. It was thought that jewellery made from nicker seeds would keep evil at bay.

1. "Sea heart" bean
2. Oarweed
3. Nickernuts
4. Dried mango seed
5. Serrated wrack seaweed
6. "Horse eye" bean
7. Dulse seaweed

Frost on the mistletoe

As the winter day passes, you might see ghostly reminders of the cold, early morning on the ground. These frosty patches on the road show the shapes of the hedge and the nearby poplar tree. These "frost shadows" are created when the shadows of objects or plants prevent the heat of the sun from warming the ground. As the sun gradually moves across the sky, the plants' shadows will move, too, and these icy patches will then disappear.

High up in the poplar trees, the round bunches of mistletoe are starting to produce white berries. Mistletoe only grows on other plants or trees, as it takes water and nutrients from a host plant rather than source them on its own.

In the United Kingdom, mistletoe is associated with Christmas, and is often hung in people's homes during the holiday. Traditionally, it is a sign of friendship as well as of love and fertility. When caught under the mistletoe with someone else, many people offer a kiss to show their friendship or love.

A mistle thrush has spotted the white berries. As its name suggests, this bird prefers to feed on mistletoe, and will fiercely defend any berries found in its territory. Listen for its loud, whistling song in the morning, letting other birds know that this patch is taken!

Woodland fungi

The winter woodland floor is the perfect place for fungi growth. The decaying bark, decomposing fallen leaves and wet winter weather creates a damp, musty environment where fungi can thrive.

Look for bright red toadstools sprouting up among the fallen branches and leaf litter. This is "fly agaric", one of the most well-known species of fungus. It often appears in fairy tales, and has been used in many traditional religious rituals. The toadstools are the fruit of the fungus, and they can grow up to 30 centimetres (12 in.) tall and 20 centimetres (8 in.) wide. As they mature, their rounded caps get flatter and their white spots drop off.

Long-stemmed, winding toadstools grow from a fungus called "sulphur tuft". This fungus feeds off rotting wood and roots, so the toadstools are often found clustered over logs or tree stumps. They get their name from their delicate yellow colour, but they are also known as "brownies".

Both types of toadstool may look bright and attractive, but they are poisonous, so they are best left to be enjoyed by the woodland elves and fairies!

1. "The prince" mushroom
2. Bovine bolete mushroom
3. Sulphur tuft mushroom
4. Grove snail
5. Fly agaric toadstool

1

2

3

4

5

On the estuary

River estuaries in the winter may look cold and uninviting, but it is a rich paradise for wading birds! The large, shallow stretch of water is full of cockles, lugworms and other creatures that live deep in the mud and provide lots of food. In winter, high tides and floods keep the estuary mud soft and full of marine life, and hundreds of birds flock to the estuaries during the colder months to feed and roost.

Listen out for the loud "peep" of the oystercatcher. It uses its long, red bill to dig cockles out of the mud and prise open the shells. Its neighbour, the curlew, also has a bill designed for digging deep. The curlew's thin, curved bill helps it to hook worms and shrimps out of the ground.

The little dunlin is a new arrival, and has come to spend the winter at the coast. In the summer, dunlins nest in upland moors and bogs, where they mate, lay eggs and raise their chicks. During breeding season, their feathers are red, brown and black, but now, as they return to the estuary, their grey-and-white winter plumage has grown in.

1. Curlew
2. Oystercatcher
3. Redshank
4. Dunlin
5. Brent goose

The winter garden

It looks very bare in the garden. The growing cycle for many plants and trees is over – their flowers have bloomed, their fruits have been seeded and their leaves have been lost. Winter is the time for these plants and trees to shut down and conserve their energy until the warmer weather returns, and they can begin their growth cycle again.

However, there are some rebel plants in this garden that do not follow the trend. The yellow witch-hazel flowers are blooming brightly, and the pale, delicate petals of the wintersweet plant open to reveal the dark buds inside.

There may be fewer insects around to visit these flowers at this time of year, but there is also less competition from other flowering plants. The few bees and moths that are still out and about will visit the witch hazel and wintersweet to feed on their nectar. By flowering now, these plants have an advantage as they are the only food option for pollinating insects. As the insect feeds on the flower's nectar, it also collects a dusty material, called "pollen", on its body. When the insect visits another flower, it transfers the pollen, and this helps the plant to develop fruit and seeds.

Food is also scarce for many other animals and birds at this time of year. Humans help by hanging feeders on their balconies and in their gardens, keeping them filled up with tasty nuts and seeds.

A winter's night

Winter is the perfect time to gaze up at the stars. During this season, the nights are long and it gets dark earlier than at any other time of year. This is because the northern half of the earth is tipped away from the sun, so it receives less of the sun's light.

In addition, the sky is now at its clearest. Cold temperatures mean that the air holds less moisture in the winter than in the summer. When it is warm, the air is often hazy with moisture and cloud. However, in the winter weather, the sky stays clear of cloud cover and the stars and planets can appear as defined, sharp lights in the night sky.

The moon is also at its highest and brightest at this time of year. Although the earth changes position as it moves around sun, the moon's position as it moves around the earth does not change. It stays on the same journey, or "orbit", all year round.

This tilting of the earth means that in the summer, when the northern half of the planet is tipped towards the sun, the sun will appear at its highest point in the sky and the moon appears at its lowest. So, in the winter, when the earth is tipped away from the light and the sun is low during the day, you should be able to look up at night and see the moon shining high in the sky.

Holly and ivy

Evergreen plants bring a welcome splash of colour to the sparse winter landscape. Unlike deciduous plants that lose their leaves in the winter, evergreens like ivy and holly keep their green leaves all year round.

Plants rely on sunlight to help them make their food, in a process called "photosynthesis". This involves a chemical called "chlorophyll", which is in the plants' leaves and produces their green colour. In winter, the shorter daylight hours means that some plants are not able to easily create food. Deciduous plants therefore stop the production of chlorophyll, shed their leaves and "go to sleep" until spring.

However, most evergreen plants have special leaves that are tough and waxy. This type of leaf helps to keep in moisture and cope with colder conditions so evergreen plants don't need to shed their leaves during the winter. This ivy plant will continue to absorb the winter sunlight when it can, while it waits for the warmer days to return.

Some evergreen plants also produce a welcome source of food. Birds like this blackbird and robin rely on the berries of plants like holly, ivy and mistletoe during these cold months.

1. European robin
2. Common holly
3. Common ivy
4. European blackbird
5. European mistletoe

A swim to start the year

It is the first morning of the New Year. These swimmers have come down to the beach to brave the January waters. After shedding their warm coats, jumpers and shoes, they pick their way barefoot across the sand to the water's edge. They shriek at the shock of the cold water, as the first wave hits their feet and rushes around their ankles. Then they take deep breaths and wade further in, until they feel ready to take a bracing plunge into the waves.

On 1 January, new-year swims take place all over the United Kingdom. People organise swims in the sea, lakes, rivers or outdoor pools called "lidos". In some places, they jump into the water from bridges, or take their dip in fancy dress. It is seen as a fun and exhilarating way to mark the start of a new year.

Humans can only swim in cold water without protection for short periods of time. It is dangerous for humans to stay in the water for too long, as they lose too much heat through their skin. These grey seals, on the other hand, are well protected against the cold. Seals are mammals, but they can stay warm in the sea because they have a thick layer of fat under their skin, called "blubber". This keeps their bodies warm, even when they have been in the sea for hours.

The Apple Wassail

On a freezing January night, groups of people gather in orchards around the country to celebrate a particular tradition. A Wassail Queen, wearing a crown, will lead a parade of people through the apple trees towards the oldest tree in the orchard.

When she arrives at the tree, she soaks a piece of toast in mulled cider – a warm alcoholic drink made from apples, sugar and spices. Then, she hangs the soaked toast from one of the tree's branches. Further pieces of toast are hung from the tree as mulled cider is poured around its trunk. The crowd then bangs sticks and drums to scare away evil spirits. Everyone sings a song to the orchard, wishing the trees a good, healthy year of growth.

This is the Apple Wassail, an English custom that has taken place in apple orchards for centuries. It began as both a celebration and a way to bless the trees and make sure that they produced lots of fruit in the coming year.

Apples are native to the United Kingdom, and they were an important source of food for people in the past. They remain popular fruits because they can be stored for months, cooked in many different ways, used to make cider or simply eaten raw.

Dark mornings

January can feel like a long, dark month. Even though the shortest day of the season has already passed and the days are starting to get longer, the times of the sunrise and sunset do not change at the same rate. For a while, the sun sets a few minutes later at the end of the day, but it continues to rise at around the same time every morning. This means we carry on getting ready for school and work in the dark.

This happens because the earth is slightly tilted, and because its journey, or "orbit", around the sun is an ellipse – a shape rather like an oval – rather than a perfect circle. The earth moves faster at the point in its orbit where it is closer to the sun. This, combined with its tilt, pushes the earth's "solar time" out of sync with our clocks. It happens every year in early January, and means that for a few days, dawn seems to stand still.

Most animals and birds rely on the natural cycle of light and dark. Many birds will not wake and sing until dawn arrives, meaning that the time they are awake and able to find food is shorter. On the other hand, nocturnal animals who are awake at night, such as foxes, have much longer to hunt in these dark days.

An icy dip

On cold days, when the air temperature drops below zero degrees Celsius (32°F), the water on the surface of this pond may freeze into floating sheets of ice. However, the waterbirds that live here, such as mallards and coots, simply swim around the icy patches.

At first glance, it looks like the birds' thin webbed feet have no protection against the winter conditions, as the feet have no fat or feathers to protect them against the cold. However, they have a secret weapon to stop them losing heat as they paddle about.

The arteries and veins that carry blood to and from a waterbird's feet are set close together inside their body. Warm blood is pumped from the heart through the arteries, and cold blood returns from the feet through the veins. As the warm blood passes the cold blood, heat is transferred from one to the other. The cold blood returning to the body is warmed up, and the warm blood going to the feet becomes cooler. So, by the time the blood reaches the bird's feet, there is less heat left in the blood to lose.

With this clever system, coots, mallards and other waterbirds are able to keep their body heat away from the water, which means that they stay warm, even on the chilliest of swims.

Making a mark

These children were up early this morning, eager to play in the fresh fallen snow. However, some other creatures got there before them! A snowy day provides a great opportunity to log the activity of local wildlife. Can you see the tracks across the snow? They tell us who has been out and about and where they have been going.

This dog's footprint is made up of a large pad and smaller toes. It is similar to a wild fox print, but a fox's is narrower and the toes are closer together, so it looks more like a diamond in shape.

The two long, thin prints beside two short ones belong to a rabbit. A rabbit's hind feet are much longer than its front feet. You will often see sets of these tracks crossing each other, as rabbits are social and tend to stick together.

Can you see the smaller twig-like prints? A wren has hopped through the snow, hoping to find an insect or spider on the ground to snap up. These tracks stop suddenly, showing where the wren took flight.

The tiny set of footprints running about show that a mouse has also visited the park, darting across the snow before returning to the safety of its nest.

Preparing the fields

As the winter moves on, farmers begin to get ready for the arrival of spring. Soon it will be time to plant crops for the start of the next growing year.

In order to give their plants the best conditions to grow in, farmers must prepare the soil. Plants do not just use the soil as a place to live – they draw minerals and nutrients from the soil through their roots to help them grow.

These fields have been ploughed and left empty all winter. This allows the soil time to rest and recover from last year's harvest. However, it still needs a little help to get all its nutrients back, as they were absorbed by last year's crop. To speed up the process, farmers will often sprinkle slurry on the fields to enrich the soil before planting.

Slurry is a liquid made from animal waste and crop waste that has been mixed together and made into fertilizer. It may smell pretty bad, but it has lots of nitrogen and potassium in it – two of the most important elements of healthy soil. Spreading it over the fields now means that the spring plants will have a rich source of food.

Picnic at the rowan tree

It is busy by the rowan tree, as its bright, red berries entice a lot of birds to visit. The fieldfare, goldcrest and blue tit here are making the most of the late rowan berries, which are a rare source of food in the bare winter landscape.

Birds like these will eat as many berries, seeds and other foods as they can find during the winter days. This helps birds to build the necessary fat and energy reserves to keep warm during the long, cold nights. Groups of birds are also more likely to feed and sleep together during the winter, helping them to keep warmer as well as to protect themselves from predators.

Late winter also welcomes some of the early signs of spring, as the rowan tree starts to produce small, hairy buds. In spring, these buds will become clusters of white flowers. After insects have pollinated the flowers, the trees will be able to produce berries in autumn, and the cycle begins again.

The rowan tree is also sometimes known as the "witch tree". Historically, its red berries were thought to provide excellent protection against evil. Because of this superstition, the trees were often planted next to houses as a way to scare off any witches who might be tempted to visit.

1. Bullfinch
2. Goldcrest
3. Fieldfare
4. Blue tit
5. Redwing
6. Waxwing

Morning mist

As the sun rises, a layer of mist hangs over these fields, wrapping itself around the trees and houses.

Morning mists like this can often be seen in winter. They happen when warmer water in the air cools rapidly, causing it to change from invisible gas to tiny water droplets. As the day progresses and the sun moves further overhead, the air heats up again. The droplets then evaporate and become gas, and the mist vanishes.

Since dense, cold air sits lower than warmer air, valleys between hills like this one tend to trap the mist, so the clouds appear to "sit" in the valley. The people who live here must take care, as it can be hard to see clearly when you are driving or walking about in the mist.

A short-eared owl swoops in and out of the mist on its morning hunt, looking for voles or mice in the fields. This species of owl is unusual because, unlike most of the United Kingdom's owls, it prefers to hunt in the daytime. Once this owl has found its food for the day, it will return to its nest, which is a scraped-out hole in the ground, lined with warm grass and feathers.

The first flowers

In the woodland, the first green buds are starting to push
their way up through the frosty ground. Snowdrop buds
blossom into white bells, early crocuses burst into purple
petals and lesser celandines become delicate yellow stars.
These are the first flowers of the year, and they tell us that
the temperatures are rising. Winter is coming to an end,
and spring is on its way.

These first flowers are an important source of nectar for
insects emerging from hibernation. This early bumblebee
queen has spent most of the winter asleep in a small hole in
the ground. Now she is awake, she must find somewhere to
make a nest and lay her eggs, and she must also build up a
store of nectar. The food she can find in these early flowers
will help her to begin this task.

This stoat is shedding his white winter coat, and his summer
fur is starting to grow. Now that the snow and frost are
almost gone, his white coat won't provide camouflage when
he sneaks across the ground in search of mice and birds to
eat. His brown summer coat is a better disguise when the
warmer weather comes.

1. Snowdrop
2. Lesser celandine
3. Early bumblebee
4. Early crocus
5. Stoat

Floods

This place has undergone a huge transformation. It is a floodplain – an area of land next to a river that stretches from the river's banks to the sides of the river valley. Most of the time, the land remains above water and is used for growing crops and pasturing animals. The fence posts show where the field's boundaries are usually marked. However, at times of high water, a river might burst its banks, causing the plain to flood.

Floods are more common during wintertime. They can be caused by a number of things: heavy rainfall or melting ice and snow can swell rivers with water and overload drainage systems, or winter storms and high sea tides can stop river water from flowing out into the sea, so it is pushed back into the river's mouth.

Floods can cause power cuts and damage to homes and businesses but, despite this risk, floodplains are often used for farming and building, because the soil is good for crops and the flat land is easy to build on.

For these herring gulls, the flood makes a welcome change. This species of bird hunts for fish and other marine life in bodies of water, and the flood has dramatically expanded their hunting ground. See how they circle above the water, looking for their next meal.

Below the surface

At the surface this pond looks calm, but down here new life is beginning. This translucent clump of dotted jelly is actually frogspawn, the eggs of the common frog. The female lays her eggs, and the male fertilizes them as they emerge. The frogspawn then mature and grow in size, until each egg is ready to hatch into a tiny black tadpole.

The tadpoles swim around the pond, black tails flicking back and forth, feeding on algae and the old jelly from the frogspawn to help them grow. Later in the spring, their tails will gradually disappear and they will develop legs, but for now they are only at the start of their journey.

Toads also reproduce in this way. However, they lay their spawn in long chains rather than big clumps.

It may seem like there are a lot of tadpoles here for just one pond, but this is not unusual, because early life is dangerous for frogs. It is estimated that only one in fifty tadpoles will reach adulthood, because many different birds, fish and other creatures, including the great crested newt, prey on them. Therefore, frogs need to lay a lot of eggs to make sure enough will survive into adulthood to begin the cycle again.

A Ladybird Book

collectable books for curious kids

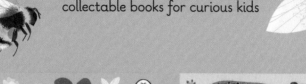

What to Look For in Spring

9780241416181

What to Look For in Summer

9780241416204

What to Look For in Autumn

9780241416167

What to Look For in Winter

9780241416228